Thoughts
Anything
and
Everything

CHARLIE ROSE

abbott press®

A DIVISION OF WRITER'S DIGEST

Abbott Press books may be ordered through booksellers or by contacting:

Abbott Press
1663 Liberty Drive
Bloomington, IN 47403
www.abbottpress.com
Phone: 1-866-697-5310

ISBN: 978-1-4582-1168-2 (sc)
ISBN: 978-1-4582-1167-5 (e)

Library of Congress Control Number: 2013916986

Printed in the United States of America.

Abbott Press rev. date: 01/24/2014

Table of Contents

CHAPTER 1

Introduction

"I think therefore I Am," is an old quotation.

I am conscious and have been given the ability to think sounds much more to the point.

The difference between animals and humans is our given ability to think and recognize ourselves.

Why is that so?

Natures Law of Change says we either increase our ability to think or Nature drops us by the wayside.

Speaking of consciousness, at ninety-six I am getting a bit forgetful. If there are any duplications in this book I shall claim it helps emphasize a subject.

At the end of chapter four is a graph showing how active consciousness fits into the scheme of things.

Natural Law applies positive energy and pushes us up the spectrum of consciousness.

Natural Law should be taught in every grade of our schools and colleges.

Life is a continuous process of learning.

We are a product of our ancestors and our own efforts. Just think of the possibilities.

What do you see when you look into a mirror?

Cause or Effect?

Acquiring new knowledge is an endless process.

It is one of the Natural Laws motivating this Universe.

You decide if the following stories are true.

Number One

Eons in the past an ancient civilization came to an impasse.

The Universe was coming to an end.

Being super conscious entities, they had acquired all possible knowledge of there time and knew how to use it.

They decided to create a new and better Universe with much more new knowledge available.

If you want to know how they made consciousness appear out of a huge explosion, you will have to ask them or figure it out for yourself.

Number Two

Far out on an arm of one of the billions of Galaxies that make up our Universe is a small planet called Earth.

Walking on the surface of this Earth is a human brain capable of thinking its own thoughts.

Inside that brain is a conscious individual trying to figure out why things are like they are.

That individual is Me-Charlie Rose.

I think one story is just as fantastic as the other.

What do you think?

Sooner or later we wake up and learn who we are.

Who, what, when, where and why?

We find out the future is staring us in the face at one time or another.

Opportunity knocks on our door.

Let us welcome it with open arms.

Knowledge is the key to the future. The final tally will be determined by knowledge.

CHAPTER 2

Thinking

How can I learn to think better?

If I could learn to think better, I have plenty of problems to spread it around on.

It has been said quote, "The human brain is capable of thinking anything about everything."

Sounds easy?

Have you tried positive thinking?

It turns out to be a tough job.

Maybe that is why so many people avoid it.

What has words to do with peoples thinking?

Do we let words shape to much of our thoughts?

There are thousands of words in Webster's dictionary.

Have you ever counted the words in your vocabulary?

Do not do it or you will be disappointed.

We use word pictures to try to get other people to understand what we are thinking.

The trouble with word pictures, they end up with too many unfilled blank places.

Who, what, when, where and why can be used to approach any subject.

Who am I?

What am I doing here?

When did everything around me get started?

Where am I?

Why am I here?

These are first prize winning questions that call for more questions.

I am beginning to like this idea of asking myself questions more all the time. My thinking can go anywhere and everywhere.

Take a look at politics.

Why not let the two old political parties keep mussing and fussing with each other and start a neutral common sense party to represent the silent majority in this country. A single voice cannot be heard against an organized group.

Such a party would give the silent majority a voice to contend with all the organized groups in this country, including the lobbying part of our government.

Using the five words mentioned above and some of Thomas Paines ideas, should get the Party started.

Being a common sense party it should attract more common sense members than crackpots and know it alls.

"The 5W Party" might be a suitable logo.

Our political system could use a lot more common sense in its activities.

If such a party comes along they will find plenty of members and plenty of problems.

Questions! Questions! Questions to ask yourself!

Why has our society let money get us into so much trouble?

We use four wheels to move ourselves around. Why do they cost so much?

With all the artificial drugs we have today, why are the number of ill people increasing?

Today's students grow into tomorrow's citizens. Tomorrows citizens determine the future of our country.

Why is our school budget so puny compared to other budgets of our government?

Are we such a stupid civilization, that we have to put up with the one percent and ninety-nine percent situation that we find ourselves in today?

Bring our problems out into some fresh air.

CHAPTER 3

Our Universe

Evidence points to a single Creator of this Universe.

Is our Creator a Super conscious Entity we call God?

If there is only one Creator, why are there so many different religions?

Is this Universe a thought in our Creators mind?

If that is so I am a part of this Universe, therefore, I am a part of God's thought.

Somehow that is very comforting.

How can I describe this Universe using words?

There is no law against trying.

Everything has a beginning.

Our scientist's tell us this Universe started as a huge explosion called a Big Bang.

Even for a fire cracker to explode somebody has to light the fuse.

That indicates some kind of super conscious Entity has caused the Big Bang to happen.

The explosion turned into a globe of extremely hot pure positive energy.

That changed to inertia energy and expanded rapidly.

Our scientist's tell us our Universe is still expanding today.

If that is so, everything from the smallest to the largest is in some kind of motion. The smallest particles vibrate.

Time has been a mystery from our beginning and still is.

Motion and time are two parts of the same thing. You cannot have one without the other.

If motion speeds up, time slows down. If motion slows down time speeds up.

Example: to go

10 miles at 10 m.p.h. (motion) requires 1 hour (time)
10 miles at 600 m.p.h. (motion) requires 1 minute (time)

Does the smallest unit of time determine the speed of light?

Our scientist's tell us if we travel at the speed of light we would not age.

At that speed the time element must be so small, change does not have time to take place.

Motion and time create change.

Change is a Universe absolute.

We either take advantage of change or change takes advantage of us.

If we take advantage of change we can change our future.

This idea needs to be applied to our present day monetary problems.

Change gives us the impression that time passes.

The Law of Opposites permeates our whole Universe.

The primary example is positive and negative energy patterns.

All electro-magnetic phenomena depend on opposite poles or polarity.

Every atom has a positive center and a negative electron cloud to balance it.

Inertia expands, gravity draws back.

For the Earth to stay in its orbit inertia and gravity are exactly balanced.

There are other examples of opposites to numerous to mention.

It even enters the human sphere as male and female.

CHAPTER 4

This Book

Consciousness is the subject of this book.

At the end of this chapter is a graph of a spectrum to measure active consciousness, which is a much higher form of energy than the electromagnetic spectrum.

On the bottom rung of this spectrum is the first sign of order in this Universe.

The top end is unlimited. My visualization of the top end is a Super Conscious Entity called God.

I place the best human brain at about half way up the spectrum.

In our schools today, the left brain oriented individuals that think with words can remember more of the words. Teachers say these individuals will be found at the top of the class.

Right brain oriented students that think in pictures cannot remember words, so will find themselves in the lower half of the class.

I am a right brain oriented person. Because of my poor memory for words, there will be duplication in this book.

I will claim duplication is to increase and emphasize the subject.

If reality is composed of all types of positive and active consciousness, that fact would answer a lot of unanswered questions today.

If I try to think how far a thought can be expanded, I end up with a large question mark.

Just what is a thought anyway?

If there is no such thing as nothing, thought has to be made out of something.

Consciousness keeps getting more interesting all the time.

The goal of life is proving to be increased consciousness.

Increasing our knowledge is the only way up the consciousness spectrum.

Dear reader, please bear with me in my feeble attempt to describe a part of reality with words.

Do not forget you have the same privilege and opportunity.

Spectrum of Consciousness

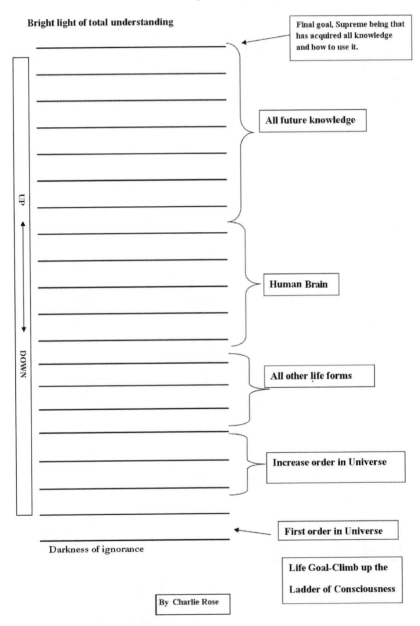

Bright light of total understanding

Final goal, Supreme being that has acquired all knowledge and how to use it.

UP

DOWN

All future knowledge

Human Brain

All other life forms

Increase order in Universe

First order in Universe

Darkness of ignorance

Life Goal-Climb up the Ladder of Consciousness

By Charlie Rose

CHAPTER 5

Active Consciousness

Sooner or later most people start thinking about things other than themselves.

Five words are enough to get most people started thinking.

Who, what, when, where and why.

Just who am I?

What am I here for?

Where are we headed?

Why are we here, anyway?

Things cannot happen without a reason.

Whose reasoning is behind reality?

Any type of order indicates some kind of consciousness behind it inducing it to do so.

Active consciousness powered by positive energy seems to be the reactive force behind all reality.

People should be pursuing increased knowledge as diligently as they do money today.

Increased consciousness is the only thing we can take with us when we leave this Earth, that means the proper use of positive and negative energy patterns today.

See graph of spectrum to measure active consciousness at end of Chapter 4.

I propose to design a graph showing a spectrum that will measure active consciousness patterns, which are composed of much higher energy patterns than electro-magnetic waves with its own spectrum.

For more detail see active consciousness graph at the end of Chapter 4. It shows how active consciousness fits into the scheme of things.

To create motion and action, active consciousness has to use positive energy patterns.

To help us visualize reality, more detail is needed.

Our scientist's tell us this Universe started with a huge explosion called the Big Bang.

Even for a fire cracker to explode somebody has to light the fuse.

That means a Super Conscious of some kind had to make the Big Bang happen.

It quickly became a large globe of very hot positive energy that expanded rapidly.

Something odd here, to obey the Law of Opposites, an equal amount of negative energy patterns has to be somewhere to make things balance and make positive energy flow in the right direction, from positive to negative.

Perhaps dark matter and dark energy could be classed as negative energy patterns.

The Creator of this Universe had to obey Natural Laws laid down by a still higher authority to get the job done.

Natural Law makes this Universe proceed in an orderly fashion.

If people obeyed all the Natural Laws, they would have no problems or troubles.

Natural Laws should be taught in every grade of our schools. At least people would know how to think better.

One of the Natural Laws is the Law of Opposites.

The Law of Opposites permeates our entire Universe.

A magnetic field has to have two opposite poles, every atom has a positive center and a negative cloud of electrons around it, for the Earth to stay in orbit. Positive inertia and negative gravity have to exactly balance.

A flow of energy can produce all kinds of cyclic activity.

Our life span has a beginning and an ending and leaves something to repeat the cycle.

All wave forms are cyclic in nature.

The Big Bang produced Galaxies. Galaxies produce suns, suns produce sun light, sun light produces plant life. Our brain uses energy from plant life to think with. Positive thoughts push us up the ladder of consciousness. Where does the cycle end?

The same type of energy lifts our foot and moves it, so we can walk on this Earth. Gravity pulls our foot back down and keeps us from flying off into space.

Why is a troublesome word!

Have you asked yourself why we are here?

I think we were put here to be healthy and happy and enjoy life.

If we are not we must be braking some Natural Law.

Ask yourself why you have been given the ability to laugh.

Just why are we here anyway?

There are few clues.

Nature has experimented for over a billion years to produce a brain capable of abstract thinking.

It is also called evolution.

Nature's experimenting has put us in our present place on the spectrum of consciousness.

By giving us a brain to think with, Nature has given us the job of using positive thoughts to push ourselves up the ladder or suffer the consequences.

That means our life goal is increased consciousness.

Now is the time to take advantage of change and use positive energy patterns to solve the problems that plague our civilization today and push us up the ladder.

Motion and time create change.

Change is a Universal absolute.

Time is a continuous now subject to change.

We make our own future individually and collectively.

Change does not let the human race stay in one place.

Do you think you are smarter than your stone-age ancestors?

If we take advantage of change we can change our future.

That brings up the subject of money.

A complete book could be written about the use and abuse of money.

Money is mans invention and subject to mans whims and thinking.

Constant thinking about money seems to hold our civilization at one place on the spectrum of consciousness.

The Law of change says we cannot stay in one place.

We either solve our problems and move further up the spectrum or suffer the consequences and back down.

To find an answer examine the antics of all our financial institutions that handle other people's money.

We either use positive thinking to push us toward the light of understanding or we stay in the darkness of ignorance.

About eighty years ago a teacher gave me a gem of wisdom and I quote, "It is easy to be a dummy, all you have to do is do nothing."

Same with getting something for nothing.

Nature says, "there is no such thing as a free lunch."

Is that why people using other people's money have created such huge debts everywhere?

How many people know that if they obeyed Natural Laws, the dark clouds would part and the light of understanding would shine through.

If you are looking for a tough job, try changing people's way of thinking and acting.

I keep asking myself questions and sometimes I find an answer.

At least it gives me a chance to be more aware of my surrounding and try to do something about it.

Why is the Earth, a tiny speck in the scheme of things the only place in this Universe we find life and active consciousness. They must go together.

Is consciousness trying to express it's self. Should that be civilizations goal for each of us.

Only fools make life's goal piling up large sums of money.

Today the only thing between us and utopia is the way we think.

CHAPTER 6

Gravity

Gravity is mysterious stuff.

Humans have much to learn about gravity.

Every atom and group of atoms, including individuals, broadcast their own unique gravity wave form that spreads outward in all directions at the speed of light.

They fill the whole Universe and when they reach the outer limits, they keep right on going uncovering more passive consciousness space.

Space is the media that electro-magnetic waves travel in.

Our Creator uses gravity wave forms to be aware of any spot anywhere in the Universe at anytime.

Gravity and inertia keep order amongst all the larger components of this Universe.

Gravity could be one of the more subtle energy patterns created by the Super Consciousness behind all order that makes this Universe what it is.

CHAPTER 7

Homo Sapiens

It has taken Nature a billion years to produce a brain capable of abstract thinking.

That is why we call ourselves human beings and are aware of being so.

Everything in this Universe is controlled by Natural Laws.

Any breaker of a Natural Law pays the penalty doing so, no exceptions.

As a species we do not seem to have learned that lesson yet.

Let us look at 5000 years of man's religious ideas.

Where are we today?

All God like activity is positive in nature.

Do you think killing each other, piling up weapons of all kinds, including atomic bombs, and the creating mayhem of all kinds is God like qualities?

By the way how many atomic bombs would it take to blow us back to the stone-age?

Let every Man and Woman on this Earth think that over. Remember you have a vote.

How about another side of the picture?

The one percent and the 99 percent or a few billionaires and the large mobs of hungry people.

If we want to climb the spectrum, we better get busy.

Homo sapiens have been given the ability and the tools to make this Earth a paradise for every one of us.

It cannot be done using a few billionaires and large groups of hungry people. The only way is the use of positive thinking or obeying Natural Laws.

Change is an absolute of this Universe.

Change is a product of motion and time.

We have been given the ability to take advantage of change.

This means we have some control of our future.

This idea should be applied to our money problems today.

Perhaps the only way is to start with our youngest ones and teach them all about positive and negative thinking and all of our Natural Laws in every grade of our schools. By that time maybe all of our citizens would know how to think properly for themselves. A plus for everyone.

We have one life to live and we are all in the same boat.

For anything to happen there has to be a reason.

If Nature experimented with living species for a billion years, she must have been looking for something.

The most oblivious denominator is increased consciousness.

To me that indicates the goal of life is increased consciousness and how to use it.

As soon as Homo sapiens were able to do abstract thinking, our species was the only ones that has managed to spread over the entire surface of the Earth.

Today other species are disappearing as if nature is done with them.

Nature has pushed the human species about half way up the spectrum of consciousness. It is now man's job to push himself the rest of the way.

He now teaches himself how to act and think using positive energy or else!!!

I do not think nature puts all her eggs in one basket.

I will bet a dollar to a donut, there are other types of life set up to accomplish the same thing we are supposed to do here on Earth. We would call them Aliens.

CHAPTER 8

Transportation

Along about 1910 a man built and sold a four wheeled vehicle called a Model T for about $300. ($3000 in today's cheap money)

This Model T helped end the horse and buggy era, changed people's way of thinking and speeded up people's way of doing things.

Now 2012 do you suppose our college trained engineers have learned enough in 100 years to build a vehicle for $8000 or $9000 to do the same thing the Model T did—change people's thinking and get the lower half of our work force moving again. This vehicle would be mainly for short trips.

Today's vehicle is a holdover from the 20th century, when we had oil to waste.

Today's car costs too much, weights too much, wastes too much of our precious gasoline and precious raw materials.

Today's car buyers are supposed to think of cars as a prestige symbol.

The problems with today's cars are obvious, even bridges have to be built to carry twice the weight they should have to.

If we do not use common sense the opposite of common sense will happen to us.

Change is a Universe absolute.

Change that fits everyone should be our goal.

A vehicle to fit today's needs is called for.

I will call my attempt to describe such a vehicle a twin model.

To start at the end of a twin models life, there should be a salvage system to recycle used wore out twin models.

I propose a gold card that stays with the title of each car.

This card would be worth the down payment on a new twin model if the old one is turned in for salvage.

Aluminum does not rust and its' characteristics makes it easy to salvage.

This car would be mostly aluminum with a steel frame.

No compound curves are needed.

Parallel sides, the square interior seems roomier.

Stream lined front to back and top to bottom.

One foot thick foamed aluminum shock absorbing bumpers front and back for increased safety.

The entire vehicle has a flat floor, no humps.

Sixty inch tread for stability.

Collapsible steering column.

Hand cranked flat windows. The cost of electric will surprise you for no more than used.

Windshield and all windows flat safety glass.

Five inches of foam rubber on dash and back of front seat for increased safety.

Two inches of insulating foam lines entire interior of vehicle forming quieter ride and insulating qualities.

Wheels designed for least possible sprung weight for best riding qualities.

Brake drums and differential attached directly to frame of car.

The idea of simplicity has disappeared from today's car designers and engineers.

How about a vehicle to move people instead of a moving status symbol?

The designing of this vehicle should keep easy salvaging in mind.

Internal combustion engines will be used until better batteries appear in the market place.

The electrics in hybrids just adds cost and complexity to the problem.

The vehicles weight and engine characteristics are the biggest factors that determine a vehicle's miles per gallon.

The present goal should be 100 miles per gallon.

There is a two cycle engine design on the drawing board today that might be a big step toward that goal.

Compared to an iron four cylinder four cycle engine, an aluminum two cycle two cylinder engine of about the same horse power is about half as high, half as long, one-third the weight and about half the moving parts, no pop up valve trains.

There would be no water, water jacket, radiator, water pump or fan belt.

All the above waste gasoline.

Two small fans cool the aluminum engine. Fast warm up and these same fans would quickly heat the interior of the vehicle on a cold morning, no extra heater would be needed.

The geometrics of this two cycle design would be easy to work with to reach best efficiency.

Modern technology makes this new design work where older two cycle engines did not.

Why isn't this two cycle design being put together and tested for possibilities today?

Money, old age, greedy people, resistance to change, same old, same old! You name it.

Maybe this would be a good project for young college engineers with new ideas such as redesign the speedometer for increased miles per gallon and increased safety.

Such a vehicle would certainly make a change in the lower half of our work force.

This vehicle or one like it will never appear on the market unless people demand it. If you know human nature the answer is obvious.

Today each person or groups of people all look after their own pocket books.

I heard a casual observation once, "The end of our civilization will be caused by greedy people." What do you think?

Our civilization depends on energy dug out of the ground.

The end of oil is insight.

Who cares?

What has happened to common sense?

I say extreme conservation is indicated. What do you say?

CHAPTER 9

Money

What do people think about most of the time?

MONEY!

Maybe money should be a World religion. It seems to hold people's attention.

Money started out innocent enough.

People traded goods to have something different to use.

Then somebody figured their commodities were worth a certain amount of gold or silver and it could be carried in your pocket.

Then people called bankers showed up to handle peoples money.

Some bankers found out people would accept pieces of paper with numbers on it, so they would not have to carry heavy metal around.

It became easy to put any number on a piece of paper.

As long as people keep thinking pieces of paper are the same as real money, everything seems to be hunky dory.

Today paper money is printed by the ton. I call it funny money.

When money flows freely amongst all the people, we call it prosperity.

However, there is always somebody who thinks he has to be top dog and pile all the money in one place, just because our society permits it.

When that happens money cannot circulate.

It acts like a cancer on our monetary system.

Cancers only goal in life is to get bigger, regardless of the consequences.

People do not seem to realize all they take with them into the next life is increased consciousness.

There is something happening today, that has acted like an epidemic.

Cities, states and countries all over the world are afflicted and individual people, also.

It is called debt.

It acts like it is contagious and no cure has been found for it yet.

People do not seem to realize that if debt is paid off instead of increasing, huge gobs of stress could be gotten rid of. Spending other people's money seems to be too easy to do.

Money is strictly man's invention.

He has not learned how to use it successfully yet.

There was no such thing as money till man appeared on the scene.

Money does not appear in Nature's scheme of things.

Looking back at a billion years of evolution, the only stimuli that stands out is increased consciousness.

Many different species have disappeared in the past.

The human race is the only one that has spread over all the Earth's surface.

Today other species are disappearing at an alarming rate.

Man is the only species that dirties his own nest. He even pollutes the air he has to have to stay alive.

The time has come to establish a world currency that men or groups of men cannot change the value of.

Stop all wars on this planet.

Change our military budget to education. Education shapes and forms our future citizens. Our future citizens determine how we fit into the future scheme of things.

World religions are not changing man's consciousness fast enough to meet today's needs.

We must learn to obey Nature's Laws or pay the consequences. Look at our troubles today.

That is why Nature's Laws should be taught in every part of our educational system.

The right use of change is mandatory to advance our civilization.

As a species we cannot stand still.

Nature's constant change dictates we either climb up the spectrum of consciousness or we slide back.

That means we learn all there is to know about positive and negative force field patterns and how to apply them successfully to our everyday lives.

Look around you, what do you see?

Then ask yourself, "How stupid can we get?"

Today's money problems are keeping us from climbing the spectrum ladder.

Increased consciousness is one answer to the problem.

It gives us the ability to take advantage of change, an absolute of this Universe. This is our home, the only known home we will ever have for all the people.

Do you suppose Mother Nature is proud of her homo sapiens and their house keeping?

CHAPTER 10

More Thoughts

A wise man has said, "I think therefore I am."

If all I am is what I think, I better get busy.

Sounds easy!

When I think of all the things I can think about, it is like opening a Pandora box.

Seems like I can only think of one thing at a time, which does not help much.

Nature has given us a brain to think with, but not many instructions as how to use it.

That must be why so many people think in such a willy nilly fashion.

I have tried constructive thinking.

It turns out to be a tough job.

That must be why so many people avoid it.

Just what are thoughts anyway?

That is a first prize winning question.

The dictionary says thought is the result of thinking.

So much for that.

Our scientists say thought is a group of electrons jumping from one brain cell to another inside of our skulls.

Do you believe that?

I think our consciousness creates thoughts to help us make sense of nonsense or bring order out of disorder.

There are at least two ways of thinking:

General thoughts that cover a lot of territory.
Specific thoughts that describe the general thinking.

Most people get the two all mixed up.

Our brain has been compared to a computer.

In order for a computer to make sense out of nonsense, it has to have a programmer.

Do you suppose our consciousness is our programmer?

The positive thinkers of our civilization have established our present position on the spectrum of consciousness.

What is in the future for our civilization?

I would like to make a prediction about the human race's future.

"When our civilization reaches the zenith of its wisdom and knowledge, one of the smartest scientists, with the help of the computers of his day will figure out what active consciousness is. Consciousness will turn out to be an extremely complicated mathematical formula."

When that happens, scientists will immediately become a Super Conscious Entity.

Those Super conscious scientists have reached the top of the consciousness spectrum and will be capable of creating anything even a new Universe. End of prediction.

Even at our stage of the game Nature says, "Increased consciousness is the goal of life."

Nature has pushed us up to our present position on the spectrum. A billion year process.

It is now up to us to use our brain to climb the rest of the way up the spectrum.

There is way too much disorder in our thinking today.

Since Natural Law makes this Universe an orderly process, man should study and apply as much Natural Law to his thinking process as possible.

This is a tough assignment considering the type of people on this planet today. The news medias constant blast of negativity day after day and the TV programs fed our children at their most impressive age hour after hour only aggravate the situation.

CHAPTER 11

Time

Time has been a mystery from our beginning and still is.

Motion and time are two parts of the same thing. We cannot have one without the other.

If motion speeds up, time slows down, if motion slows down, time speeds up.

Example: MPH=miles per hour

To go 10 miles at 10 MPH (motion) requires 1 hour (time).
To go 10 miles at 600 MPH (motion) requires 1 minute (time).

Is the speed of light determined by the smallest possible unit of time?

Our scientist's tell us if we travel at the speed of light we would not age. At that speed the unit of time must be so small, change does not have time to take place.

If motion stops time stops.

Our first unit of time measured on a complete circle of the Earth around the Sun. It is called a year. For convenience that circle was chopped into smaller units—months, weeks, days, hours, minutes and seconds.

Our Earth is divided into twenty four sections. At the equator they are about one thousand miles across.

Instead of saying the Earth has turned one revolution or that we just traveled twenty four thousand miles or twenty four hours, we say a day has passed.

Time is an abstraction.

People look at a clock and think nothing about it.

Now is all there is.

A constantly changing now is caused by motion.

Past and future are only pictures in our mind to help us visualize reality.

Change is an absolute of this Universe.

Change gives us the impression that time passes.

We take advantage of change or change takes advantage of us.

Do you suppose the way energy flows from positive to negative has anything to do with the way we age.

When we start our space ship trip we are filled with energy. When we end our trip we run out of energy.

The only thing we gain is increased consciousness.

Each person's awareness of time is intimately connected to change.

Regardless of what we do each revolution of the Earth makes us one day older.

Change is one of the main absolutes of this Universe.

The flow of energy from positive to negative is the driving force behind change.

It can be written as a simple equation: Minus plus plus equals zero.

In other words our Universe is running down.

When all the positive and negative energy patterns become equal they cancel each other.

There will be one huge poof and the whole caboodle will go back to where it came from.

Change and time are immutable. If there is ever a thing called time travel it will take place in our mind and consciousness.

If motion stops we will have reached the end of our string. Nothing can happen. The energy we use to breath comes from a shining sun.

CHAPTER 12

Trees

Tall green trees are pleasing to our eyes and pleasant to be around.

Trees grow in only one place in this whole Universe, on a tiny planet called Earth.

Trees take in carbon dioxide for growth and release oxygen into the atmosphere.

Oxygen is the very breath of life.

Earth's population is growing at an alarming rate.

Men are cutting down trees as fast as they can swing a chain saw.

Cutting down trees changes the climate in a negative fashion.

To look at the overall picture, what do we see?

Ask yourself, how stupid can we get?

What is the most plentiful building material on this Earth?

SAND

We have whole desserts of sand.

Why not mix sand and the material that makes cement together and pulverize the mixture and mix in a foaming agent to make it lighter and have better insulating qualities.

38

This material would be fire proof, moisture proof, rot proof, bug proof, and rodent proof.

Pumped thru a hose and cast into any shape.

Standard molds or special ones.

This would be an excellent project for young college grads to work on.

A plant at the edge of a dessert with plenty of sunshine for energy and the process kept out of the hands of greedy people. This material could benefit flood and earth quake victims and slum dwellers of this world.

In, this day and age is that to much to hope for.

A thought about people that insist on living on river flood plains.

Why not build basements on top of the ground. Build houses on top of the basements.

Use the basement for a garage, for lawnmowers and a place the flood waters could go, thus save the stress and mess.

I might as well ask why people do like they do? There seems to be something called hard headedness.

CHAPTER 13

Space Travel

Did you know every one of us is already an astronaut?

Our space ship is a beautiful blue and white globe called Earth.

Every one of us starts the trip as equals. Male and female are just designed different to achieve different objectives.

All of us start out with a clean slate. It is what is written on this slate that causes most of our troubles.

We are also given the ability to acquire knowledge while making the trips.

Our ticket calls for one hundred trips around the Sun. One trip requires one year.

We live in a closed Universe, nothing is lost.

Nature spends nine months putting together a suitable vehicle, so our ego can live and move on the surface of our space ship.

When our ticket expires and our space ship trip ends, Nature steps in again and creates a suitable vehicle for us to use in the next environment we find ourselves in.

All we get to take with us when we make the transfer is the knowledge we acquired while making the space ship trips.

Life's goal is always toward increased consciousness.

Our scientist's tell us our space ship is traveling through space at several hundred miles per second.

The funny part is-no one seems to have the slightest idea where we are headed for.

Nature has given us the knowledge and tools to make this space ship a paradise for humans. Ask yourself why things are such a mess?

The value of anything is usually determined by its scarcity.

In this whole Universe on this tiny Earth is the only place life is known to exist. Talk about scarcity!

Look around you. What do you see?

Then ask yourself, how stupid can we get.

Think of what could be done by just changing our way of thinking.

That old adage-we take advantage of change or change will take advantage of us-is still true.

CHAPTER 14

Food

What a small word to cause so many people so much trouble.

There will soon be 7,000,000,000 people on the surface of this Earth.

That means there are seven billion stomachs that need to be filled, hopefully at least once every day.

Maybe it is a good thing we cannot look into the future. That way it is useless for us to worry about what the future is going to bring us.

Let us go back to a single person.

Enzymes are an important part of the food we eat.

Fresh harvested fruit and vegetables contain the most enzymes. I call such food live food. It spoils easily, because of the enzymes.

Heating and processing kills enzymes. Such food will set on a shelf for years without spoiling. I call such food dead food.

Eating a continuous diet of dead food is like burning cheap gas in your car. It will run but perform poorly.

To live a healthy long life, eat plenty of enzymes and drink plenty of clean energized water.

What will ten billion people do to this Earth?

To have a long healthy life span, learn all you can about enzymes.

CHAPTER 15

Nothing

Nothing is an interesting word.

A person cannot visualize nothing in his mind, only the word nothing.

According to the consciousness theory nothing does not exist.

If you create a new thought it does not come from nothing. It has to be made of something.

How could something be made from nothing?

If the law of opposites is obeyed and two Universes of opposite polarity were set up, could we say there are two Universes?

However if they came back together, poof back to nothing.

Our Universe does not expand into nothing.

Outside our Universe has to be some type of passive consciousness field that extends clear beyond our imagination.

I cannot believe we start from nothing and end up nothing.

Some type of consciousness is involved to get the job done.

CHAPTER 16

A dummy! To be or not to be?

If you want to be a dummy it is easy.

All you have to do is do nothing.

At least, that is what a teacher told me one time.

I feel sorry for teachers. They keep talking about all the dummies they have to put up with.

But then I guess some people do have an edge on being dummies.

I do think if a person is holding a couple of objects in each hand he is aware that he is holding more than one object.

We have to go to school to learn that two and two are four, four and four are eight and if we can say eight and eight are sixteen, we are suppose to be getting smarter and if we learn that X plus Y equals Z we are immediately in the smart class.

CEO's do not get paid for being dummies. I don't know just what they get paid for, just be one.

In our society anyone that piles up a bunch of money, it does not seem to make any difference how he does it, he is suppose to be a smart cookie. (No dummy!)

Just where is the dividing line between need for money and greed for money?

Mortgaging part of your future for a few more pleasures today does not work very well either.

In other words, stay out of debt and do not be a dummy.

CHAPTER 17

More Questions

Why do our scientists keep trying to find the smallest particle that exists?

If they do find it, what will they do then, twiddle their thumbs?

Our scientist's burn the midnight oil trying to figure out what consciousness is. If they would figure out what happens to the human ego when we go to sleep, the whole ball of yarn might unravel.

Just what is an energy field?

Everything in this Universe today is some type of energy pattern created by the positive energy from the big bang.

What is the difference between positive and negative energy patterns?

A bar magnet has two poles that put out two opposite magnetic fields. Those fields have to be made out of something, what is the difference?

If a bar magnet is fixed in a jig with the north pole up and another bar magnet with the north pole down and fixed so it floats in its guides, it will float in the air.

Where does the energy come from to keep the bar floating in the air against the pull of gravity? Last time I looked it is still floating. Maybe the magnetic field nullifies gravity?

Is consciousness another type of energy pattern?

Where ever there is order there has to be consciousness behind it, directing it to do so.

Evolution has given us a brain, we either use it or lose it. (increase thinking or else)

I have received my brain from my ancestors, I hope my children do a better job of using it than I have.

The human race is less than half way up the spectrum of consciousness.

Can we call God a super conscious entity at the top of the spectrum?

Does that mean we have to work toward being more God like?

The human race has much to learn about energy patterns, gravity and millions of other things that make up reality.

It's an uphill path to travel, the more I learn the more ignorant I find myself.

We have to learn everything from a standing start.

The ones that learn to be happy in the right way are the lucky ones.

CHAPTER 18

Life and Death

Life. Plus plus plus equals more plus!

Life is one of the scarcest items in our huge Universe.

That should make it one of the most precious things that can be thought of.

The time has come for our civilization to stop killing and start helping each other up the consciousness spectrum.

Tall green trees, warm sunny days, healthy happy men, women and children. That is what life is made of.

Death

Today the word death is used in the wrong context.

We live in a closed Universe.

Energy can change from one type to another type.

When all of the positive and negative energy patterns in this Universe become exactly equal they cancel each other. Minus plus plus equals zero.

Motion stops, making time stops, everything stops.

The only thing left is complete darkness and the end of the Universe.

That is the meaning of death.

Minus plus plus equals zero.

Chapter 19

Mystery

In the palm of my hand lays several kernels of oats that I have been examining for quality. I am thinking of planting a field of oats.

Suddenly I realize these oat kernels are asleep. How in the world could that be?

I realize these kernels will remain asleep until the right stimuli (moist warm earth) comes along to wake them.

At that time those oats are smart enough to grow roots down into the ground for nourishment and leaves up into the sunlight for energy to make itself grow.

Why have oats learned to grow tall stems?

The oats roots hold it in one place so it grows, the male pollen and female flower at the top of the stalk.

When the wind waves the tall stalks it scatters the male pollen all over the field fertilizing every female flower to grow more new oats. How does it happen?

Some type of consciousness directs the oats to do there thing.

The wind blowing waves in a field of oats is a beautiful sight to see.

Maybe the unused part of the human brain is asleep, just waiting for the right stimuli to come along to wake it up to grow into something more beautiful.

Dear reader, if you get one new thought from this book, I will feel well paid for my troubles. CR

CHAPTER 20

Civilization

Civilization is a general word covering a lot of territory.

Should all the people on Earth be called one civilization or should each country be considered as a separate civilization. Each country acts that way.

We know that about a dozen civilizations have already existed in the past.

Why does each one grow to a certain stage and then fade away again?

Why can't we learn from past experience and profit by their mistakes?

Seems like our civilization has to follow natural laws of plus and minus energy patterns like everything else.

One hundred thousand years ago our ancestors sat around an open fire in a cave with their crude stone tools scattered around them.

If our civilizations knowledge keeps accelerating as fast into the future as it has during the last three hundred years, what will our descendants be doing one hundred thousand years in the future?

Of course there are atomic bombs, greedy people, mental abortions, resistance to change, and even stray asteroids to contend with.

At the present time money seems to be our civilizations biggest problem.

The fact that we have a few billionaires and large companies compared to large groups of hungry people shows that we are breaking natural laws and will have to suffer the consequences.

If present trends continue, we could end up with some form of the old cast system—one percent against ninety nine percent or a few rich and many poor.

Large debts indicate a misuse of money.

Who is going to look after the people that handle large sums of other people's money, who trust them to handle it properly? We are up against the old saw, who is going to police the police?

Different languages, different religions, different national boundaries, different types of money, even different color of skin—all create groups of people who have no intentions of thinking alike.

A common currency might be the first cooperation amongst all the countries. Something that no individual or groups of men could change the value of.

Again it's questionable. The privilege of printing paper money is too much to give up.

How about a quick history of our civilization to kind of put things in perspective.

From 0 AD to about 1500 AD, superstition just about ruled our civilization.

From about 1500 to 1900 the industrial revolution was in full swing.

From about 1900 to the present day technology has come into its own. The automobile put an end to the use of horses for transportation, speeding up people's actions and thinking.

The use of the computer chip from the middle of the 20th century until today is changing peoples actions and way of thinking again. The change is taking place faster than ever.

To predict what will happen during the rest of the 21 century is an ambitious undertaking.

The present monetary situation, increase in world population, depletion of oil and precious minerals, enough fresh water for everyone, increase in world storms and Earth upheaval will make something to talk about for a long time.

Thank the powers that be that we cannot look into the future. Anything can happen.

Chapter 21

The Human Body

Who, what, when, where and why are enough words to ask myself questions about this body.

Who designed and built this body?

Why did it take so long? A billion years?

I think our Creator does not do foolish things.

For what reason was this body produced?

I think, therefore I am a conscious individual.

My consciousness resides in a brain at the top of this body.

This brain gives my consciousness the ability to think.

By our Creators efforts the human race is already about half the way up the spectrum of consciousness. (See graph at the end of Chapter 4)

Since we now have the ability of abstract thinking it is now up to us to climb the rest of the way up the spectrum.

All evidence point to increased consciousness as the goal of life.

How does age manage to affect a beautiful human body?

Each time the Earth makes one revolution we say we are a day older.

Motion is one of this Universes absolutes.

Motion seems to create time.

If motion stops time stops.

Is motion and time the main cause of why our body ages?

Positive and negative energy patterns motivate motion.

Our maker has given us a choice, we can think either way.

Positive thinking pushes us up the spectrum of consciousness, negative thinking does the opposite.

Positive thinking takes time to build up and negative thinking causes instant destruction.

A major example of negative thinking is the atomic bomb and all other destructive explosives.

By the use of seed our body follows a life cycle, from young to old over and over.

We leave a long line of ancestors behind us.

That life cycle allows us to take advantage of change, this causes us to climb up the spectrum of consciousness if we so desire.

It is a sad story today.

This Earth could be a paradise for the human race, just by changing our way of thinking.

I do not understand why so many people spend there entire lives thinking negative thoughts. Do not forget Natural Laws bring order out of disorder.

CHAPTER 22

Life

Life is just one of the mysteries of this mysterious Universe.

Life proceeds in an orderly fashion. That indicates consciousness of some kind directing it to do so. Who does that job?

I think our Creator does not do anything without a reason. What is the reason for life?

Time is ever changing now.

Life has to fit into the picture somehow.

When and how is best left to our Creator? Our own positive thinking helps.

Where life is (as far as we know) is where ever the Earth is. There are billions of galaxies in this Universe.

The Earth is in one of them.

Why life is, is something for somebody in the future to figure out.

Evolution gives us a clue.

One common denominator is increased consciousness.

Homo sapiens have been given the ability to laugh.

That indicates we are suppose to be healthy and happy while on this Earth.

If we are not, we must be breaking some of Natures Laws.

There seems to be no end to the amount of questions that can be asked about this mysterious Universe.

Life is one of the rarest things in this Universe that should make it very precious.

The way life is treated on this Earth, is it from just plain ignorance?

How can today's people's way of thinking be changed besides hitting them over the head with a 2X4 to get their attention.

Maybe it is a good subject to teach in our schools.

The problem is how to get across its importance. Nature says, climb or else!

The fact that this tiny Earth is the only known place that has developed a brain capable of abstract thinking tells us something.

Elsewhere in this book is my prediction of how this civilization today will end.

Do you think the human race is just another species to have its day and then disappear?

Or have we been set to reach a goal sometime in the future like the top of the consciousness spectrum.

Will our civilization manage to solve its problems and climb up the spectrum of consciousness or will we flub the dub and pass back to a place in the history books?

The future is up for grabs, why not grab it.

CHAPTER 23

Memory

What is memory?

Memory is a necessary part of practically all life forms.

Memory helps us realize who we are and what to do for our own benefit.

Memory is a type of energy field created by active consciousness.

No one knows what energy fields or consciousness is.

All we know is how they affect things around us.

We have inherited the ability of thinking one thought picture at a time and a short memory, which was adequate for our ancestor's time and surroundings.

Today our inherited short memory cannot handle all the detail created by our new technology and the detail is increasing all the time.

When past civilizations reached this stage and did not solve their problems they have ended up in the dust bin of history.

A dictionary is a form of slow memory, almost useless to use to solve today's problems.

We do have a chance of staying out of nature's dust bin.

Our society has invented a device called a computer chip.

Our scientist's can build a computer with unlimited memory capacity.

The problem is teaching people how to use computer memory to solve their problems creates more detail.

There is some things I want to keep repeating.

Every intelligent person on this Earth should learn all there is to know about positive thinking and negative thinking and the influence each one has on our lives and relationship with each other.

The universal law of opposites effects all action in this Universe and should be made part of the thinking picture.

The above statements are a solution to all of our problems and should be taught in every school.

Do you realize that past and present thinking has created all of our problems. Present and future thinking will have to be used to solve all of our problems.

A hat rack is not the only reason Nature gave us a brain.

CHAPTER 24

People

Today what do people think is Earth's proudest product?

More people?

There is over 7 billion people on this Earth all ready and more show up every day.

Sooner or later people will have to think about quality instead of quantity.

The Earth will only support a certain amount of people.

If each couple was restricted to two children, our population would stabilize.

When Nature hands out brains, she says use it or lose it.

There are at least four categories that can be applied to people: Spiritual, mental, emotional and physical characteristics. (see graph at this books end)

Up to about 1700 AD people expressed the physical and emotional side of their nature most of the time.

From 1700 to today, technology is forcing people to use the mental side of their nature more all the time.

However technology is just a crutch to help people climb the spectrum ladder.

Sooner or later if people keep using positive energy, they will need to start expressing higher forms of spiritual and God like qualities to reach the top of the spectrum of consciousness, where all knowledge exists and all is the bright light of understanding.

If people decide to pursue the opposite of the picture by using negative energy, the world will be at war using atomic bombs that will blow them clear back to the stone age, where they will have to start all over again.

For petes sake, why don't people start asking themselves questions and get our problems of today out in the open where they can be worked on and start with money and greedy people.

There is only one way up the ladder and that is to use positive energy.

The use of five words: who, what, when, where and why, that can be applied to any subject, might be a start.

If people do not take advantage of change now, change will take advantage of people.

What is Earth's distinction in this Universe—People!

CHAPTER 25

Questions and more questions

Can anyone ask themselves any questions?

Will asking ourselves questions increase the scope of our thinking?

Should we do our own thinking or should we let somebody else do our thinking for us?

If truth is truth, whatever a person says or thinks cannot change the truth.

There are suppose to be specialist for most anything a person can think of.

My idea of a specialist is a person that knows more and more about less and less.

To ask ourselves questions should be the other way around from specialist.

If a person's intelligence is measured by the size of his memory, why not set up a computer memory bank and list all questions in the order of a dictionary, with whatever answers are available?

New students and stymied older people could find answers and keep asking questions to add to the bank all the time.

This computer memory bank would be open to anybody and everybody any where any time.

Is it true that new lawyers are increasing in this country all the time?

I like this idea of asking myself more questions all the time.

Anybody can do it. The only limiting factor is our own imagination.

It makes me more aware of all the problems piling up around us.

When past civilizations ran into more problems than they could not solve, they are now just paragraphs in our history books.

Is that where our civilization is heading today, if we do not solve our problems?

I have heard it said that the American tax payer is a goose that lays the golden eggs.

Somebody has been swiping the eggs, the nest is practically empty.

Why is it so easy for some people to spend other people's money?

Do you know how large a pile of one dollar bills consisting of one trillion dollars would make? Probably larger than Mt. Everest and that is just one trillion.

Our National debt is beginning to look like one of our civilizations unsolvable problems.

National debt has spread over our world like an epidemic with no solution in sight.

The cliff is getting closer.

Our government has spent money for just about everything under the sun.

How about trying a new idea?

Some people talk about a billion dollars like it was peanuts.

One billion dollars for one air plane for instance.

Why not give every high school student that finishes high school $50,000 to use as each one sees fit.

Do not laugh, let us look at the whole picture.

The students could be taught the proper use of money. The foolish one could be used as examples of how not to use money.

One billion dollars divided by $50,000 would give 20,000 students $50,000 each.

I will venture to say that new ideas, new companies and increased tax base would repay the original 100 million dollars many times over.

Let us look forty years into the future.

Would you rather have spent your tax dollars for 20,000 people increasing their knowledge or one antique air plane parked in a junk yard?

Making students go into debt for an education is negative thinking.

If you do not think so, look around you, our 18 to 30 year old group is being wasted, another sign of our inability to solve our problems today.

How can people be taught the difference between positive and negative thinking?

How can people's greed for money be changed to greed for increased knowledge?

We cannot take money with us into the next life, only increased consciousness.

We either climb toward the bright light of understanding or the law of opposites say, we will stay in the darkness of ignorance.

Change is an absolute of this Universe.

Nature has given us the ability to change, change to our own advantage.

Nature does not leave her children empty handed.

Why not use it to solve our problems.

CHAPTER 26

More Thoughts to Think About

The use and application of positive and negative energy patterns motivates everything in this Universe.

Until we change the quotation, "Do thy neighbor before he does you" to "treat thy neighbor as thy self" our troubles will follow us where ever we go.

How can a person teach himself to think better?

Nature has given us a brain to think with. It is obvious nature expects us to use it.

Greed is a survival tactic handed down to us by our ancestors; it stopped being successful thousands of years ago.

You will have to spend $3000.00 every day for 100 years to spend one hundred million.

The story of a few billionaires and large groups of poor people mixed together always ends in tragedy.

God like qualities are always expressed by a flow of positive energy patterns.

The opposite is obvious.

Learning how to use positive energy patterns properly and using it to acquire knowledge gives meaning to why we are here on this Earth.

More Thoughts

Oh!!! The mystery of life, a story even Super Conscious Entities probably enjoy.

Is a beautiful flower a work of art by an unknown artist?

Flowers are tough, they grow in the strangest places.

Let us hope our civilizations is not stupid again, it has over a dozen previous civilizations to learn from.

Are our problems today just the result of immature thinking, lazy thinking, lack of imagination?

If our educational budget and our military budget were reversed, could our increased knowledge solve our problems better than what we have done today?

If we pursued increased knowledge as avidly as we do money, we would be on our way up the spectrum of consciousness.

Our present position is the result of a few of our ancestors using positive thinking and Nature's push.

The trouble with most of us today, we simply refuse to use our imaginations. We need to laugh more, it takes more energy to frown than it does to laugh.

Why waste energy?

Probably even Nature thinks life is a big joke sometimes.

Everything in this Universe is some form of energy pattern formed from the huge globe of pure energy formed by the Big Bang.

There has to be positive and negative energy patterns, because energy only flows in one direction.

Energy patterns can however change from one type to another making possible all types of natural phenomenon.

The Universal Law of Opposites has to be obeyed, that is why positive energy patterns build up and negative energy patterns tear down.

If the people running our government are suppose to represent all the people in this country, where do the lobbyist fit into the picture?

If children are the only ones that are suppose to muss and fuss with each other, our two political parties should take notice.

What can be done about the people that want to shove our national debt to our grandchildren?

In the first place all debt of any kind is the result of negative thinking.

All the governments of our world are in trouble.

Thoughts to Think About

Our ancestors developed emotions that helped them solve the problems of their times successfully or we would not be here.

Are we at least as smart as our ancestors and develop the necessary emotions to solve the problems of today and hand our children a situation they can handle in their time?

A picture of our civilization standing on top of a cliff with one foot on a banana peel looking down on a pile of extinct civilizations might be truer than we think.

Are we asleep and need to wake up or just what is the problem?

Forming a common sense political party with a 5W logo might be the first sign of waking up.

The thinking and acting that created the mess we are in is the same one we will have to use to get us out of this mess.

Changing people's way of thinking is just about the toughest job you will find anywhere.

An empty stomach will change people's mind.

No way of obtaining money legally is another.

Money started out innocent enough.

Human greed and scheming people have gotten us into our present predicament.

We are experiencing something today that has spread over the world like an epidemic.

It is called going into debt.

If a person spends all of his today's money and all the money he can mortgage his future for, where is more money going to come from?

That is the predicament that many countries in our world are in today.

These same countries are finding out that paying back borrowed money is a painful and unpleasant job and so far no solution has been found to do so.

Prosperity is money in circulation.

Everybody gets the use of some of it.

Circulating money creates jobs.

A few billionaires and large groups of hungry people is a mix that always ends in tragedy.

Ask yourself how long can over 40 million people keep living on food stamps?

Nature tells us there is no such thing as a free lunch.

Who listens to Nature anyway?

CHAPTER 27

Cosmology

Cosmology is an interesting subject. It covers a lot of territory.

Today's cosmology is about like the blind man and the elephant; it depends who you listen to.

How so ever, our civilization is running into problems today of all kinds and if we do not start solving them, cosmology will be the least of our worries.

Our problems today are mounting up faster than our ability to solve them.

When past civilizations ran into a similar situation, they were unable to solve them and are now in the dust bin of history.

Our civilization is heading in that direction today at full speed.

We do have the advantage of increased technology, such as computers and so forth. However, all that has to be used and applied to our current problems and that takes money and effort.

The use and abuse of money is our biggest problem today.

What do our most prestigious colleges and universities teach their students today?

How to solve mans problems?

Or how to squeeze more money out of the people around them?

We will not be the first civilization that bit the dust, unless we change our ways and start solving problems in a positive fashion.

If our generation keeps increasing our national debt and then dumps it on our children and grandchildren, we will be listed with the rest of the dumbest people in history.

CHAPTER 28

Questions

Humans have been given the ability to laugh.

To laugh a person has to be healthy and feel good.

If you do not feel like laughing you must be breaking some of Natures Laws.

We reap what we sow.

Have you looked at what you have sewn lately?

Consider: Do thy neighbor before he does you.

Treat thy neighbor as thy self.

Which one of those do you think is a natural law?

The spectrum of consciousness is a tough ladder to climb. When does a person start the climb, anyway? We need all the help we can get.

Nobody knows what consciousness is, why it is or where it came from.

Regardless who you are or what you think, one person's opinion is just as good as another, when it comes to consciousness.

Common sense tells us everything has to have a reason for happening.

Do you believe all our problems today are caused by the way we think?

A cancer has one objective in life. Grow bigger regardless of the consequences.

Cancer can affect all aspects of our lives. It is a tough subject to do anything about.

Do you suppose the greed for money could be classed as a cancer?

Look around you today, what else do you see.

A Presidential election is scheduled for this year.

Have you noticed what our two political parties squabble with each other about?

The time has come for a neutral common sense party to show itself.

The silent majority in this country needs a voice to contend with all the other organized groups that insist on pursuing their own interests.

Perhaps a 5W party would fill the bill.

If you do not vote you are considered one of the silent majority.

If you do not vote politics considers you a non-person.

How many other people have wondered why men spend millions of dollars for thousand dollar jobs?

Our government spends money for just about everything, why not a TV station strictly for the use of political candidates at election time.

That would give everyone in the country an equal opportunity and stop all this money hanky panky and favoritism that goes on today.

Another interesting subject is pecking order.

Is it a natural occurrence or strictly man's invention?

Take a bank CEO and a bank teller. They both handle detail for a bank. One is paid a million dollar bill and the other is paid a hundred dollar bill. Figure that one out.

Seems like all of man's institutions has to have a pecking order, some are just worse than others.

Have you tried painting a picture of reality with words?

I am willing to try.

The quest for knowledge never ends.

Evolution is one method of looking for increased consciousness.

I will call Natures constant search for increased consciousness a Natural Law.

The Law of opposites is another Natural Law.

Our Creator had to obey the Law of Opposites laid down by a higher Authority to help create this Universe.

A prime example of the Law of Opposites is positive and negative energy patterns.

Energy flows in one direction, from positive to negative.

A huge sphere of pure positive energy was created by something called the Big Bang, that is still expanding today.

There is an equal area of negative energy patterns somewhere, that balances the equation and makes the positive energy flow in the right direction.

Anything and everything in this Universe today is a product of that original sphere of pure energy, even you and me.

Are we surrounded by a pure passive type of consciousness? Does Nature tend to specifics using positive energy to activate everything of a cyclic nature? Look at a flower, it starts from a seed, grows into a beautiful bloom, then fades away leaving a seed for a new cycle. All of Nature functions in cycles; humans, the sun and the Universe.

Are cycles Natures way of taking advantage of change?

Change can be used to change our future.

Our civilizations travel down the road of life, bringing us to a deep canyon of ignorance and superstition.

The only way across is to thoroughly understand and apply positive and negative energy patterns correctly.

Greedy people and the misuse of money has pushed us clear to the edge of the cliff and negative thinking about atomic bombs and military ventures has put a banana peel under one foot.

Some of the people in the Old Testament knew all about positive and negative energy patterns, but there muscle powered technology prevented it to spread to all the people.

Today large groups of people have tried to use positive energy patters and disregard the negative energy side of the picture. This practice has left them practically defenseless.

Look around you, what have they accomplished in the last two thousand years?

Mother Nature is an impartial observer. She has given us the ability to think, it is up to us to use it to climb toward the bright light of understanding or stay in the darkness of ignorance.

As we stand at the cliffs edge, all around us are the remains of past civilizations telling us to get busy and solve our problems or else.

People do not seem to like to think and solve problems, let somebody else do it.

There is only one way across the chasm of ignorance, our civilization has to learn all there is to know about positive and negative energy patterns and how to apply and use them in the right way.

Well! Well! Well!

We reap what we sow.

It is done unto you as you believe.

Change is an option.

Truth remains truth regardless.

Life is one of the scarcest things in this Universe.

It should be most precious.

Look around you, what do you See?

Then ask yourself, how stupid can we get?

Is this life a foot race with the devil taking the hindmost?

Laughter is one of life's mysteries.

The use of positive and negative energy patterns is mandatory to our welfare when properly used.

One percent and ninety nine percent will not work.

It becomes top-heavy and topples over.

History is an excellent teacher, pay attention.

Our political system today has a distinct odor.

A common sense neutral new 5W party could open a window and improve the situation.

The school of hard knocks tells me what life is all about.

What we learn today will shape our future.

It is easy to be a dummy and fall off the cliff into who knows what, just do nothing.

Enough is enough, I have gone fishing. Fishing for something is what life is all about. C.R.

Our Choice

Our creator has given us a choice of ways to live.

We can live on the positive side of the reality line or the negative side of the reality line.

Which side do you choose to live on?

Positive Life/reality	Negative Life/reality
Love	Hate
Laugh	Frown
Happy	Sad
Prosperity	In debt
Industrious	Lazy
Need for money	Greed for money
Beautiful flowers	Dead vegetation
Enjoy good health	Sickness—miserable
Build up and increase	Tear down—destroy
Tall trees—green grass	Dead stumps—erosion--mud
Sunshine—pleasant breeze	Cloudy—smog—stormy
Good government	Bad government
Pleasant surroundings	Unpleasant surroundings
Pleasant home life	Unpleasant home life
Final results	Final results

Graph of Life

Where do you stand on this graph?

Make a mark on each line that you think shows your accomplishments or percent of it.

If each line is about the same length out to the mark—that indicates a well balanced personality.

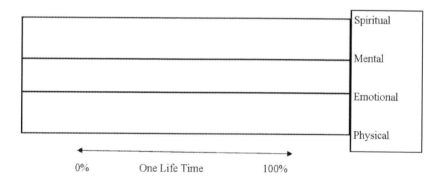

Our space ship Earth's ticket is good for one hundred trips around the Sun.

Intuition says our place in our next life is determined by what we learn and experience while making the space ship trips.

Some Observations to Think About

People make up today's civilization.

The quality of our civilization depends on how people think. To obey the Universal Law of opposites, Nature has to give us a choice, either think positively or negatively, we cannot think of both at the same time.

All God like qualities are the result of the proper use of positive thinking and action, that pushes us up the spectrum of consciousness.

The Law of Change says we cannot stay at one place on the spectrum, we are either climbing toward the bright light of increased knowledge and understanding or sliding back toward the darkness of ignorance and superstition.

Our job as a member of our civilization is to learn all there is to know about positive thinking all there is to know about negative thinking and learn the consequences of using one or the other. Words are a poor brush to paint thought pictures with.

We think thought pictures one at a time because pictures give the most detail.

Is greed an emotion inherited from our ancestors?

If so, its negative characteristics has no place in our civilization today.

It is common knowledge that prosperity depends on a flow of money for everyone.

Piling a lot of money in one place is the opposite of prosperity, because its negativity affects a lot of people. The name for it is a recession or depression.

Another negative use of money is large debts, with no solution in sight to cure it.

Nature says there is no such thing as a free lunch.

Positive energy has to be used to accomplish anything.

The whole world is on a debt binge with no solution in sight.

Maybe one reason is because it is so easy to spend other people's money.

A common currency for all people that no one could change the value of in other words, it always stays the same, is the first step up to cure our money problems.

If you are looking for a tough job, try changing human nature.

WHO WHAT
WHERE
WHEN WHY

The human brain is capable of much more than we realize, including pos
thinking. Even so, many living in today's world often struggle with maintair
an optimistic outlook in what has unfortunately become a society focused on
negative and materialism.

At ninety-six years old, Charlie Rose offers a glimpse into what he has learned ⊲
the course of a long lifetime filled with many experiences and seeks to ins
others to keep their imaginations working and minds busy creating new id
While sharing his perspective on a variety of natural laws, Rose encourages your
generations to embrace opportunities, welcome knowledge, rely on questions
stimulate more questions, take advantage of change, increase consciousness,
use positive energy to solve challenges. Included is a graph that depicts how
active consciousness fits into the scheme of life and a graph of life that illustr
accomplishments and experiences in relationship to time spent on Earth.

Thoughts Anything and Everything shares one man's thoughts with the hope th
provokes changes in thinking, new ideas, and fresh perspectives on life.

Charlie Rose was raised on a farm in the Midwest. After twelve years of educa
and eighty-five years of living, he happily shares his thoughts on the true mear
of reality. Charlie currently resides in Iowa, where he keeps busy thinking posi
thoughts every day.

abbott press®
A DIVISION OF WRITER'S DIGEST

U.S. $8.99
ISBN 978-1-4582-116

50
9 781458 211682

MÉTODO ROER 7 X 4

Método para solución de problemas empresariales y paradigmas antiguos

Ponga a prueba sus problemas delante del método Roer 7x4
Traiga su equipo de trabajo y triture sus piedras con el método Roer 7x4
Jamás dejara de utilizar este sencillo y seguro método una vez lo aprenda

Al fin llegó un práctico método para ayudar a resolver problemas

Roer en el siglo XXI, es la forma práctica, segura, eficaz, sencilla y diáfana de alcanzar el éxito en 5 pasos. Do it, very well and now.

Además de forma coherente aprenderá a tomar decisiones con su equipo de trabajo con el método de Ponderación Equivalente.

Olvídese de las tradicionales decisiones en las juntas donde prevalecen las roscas y pago de favores, decisiones sin criterio, y enfóquelos en análisis de sano entendimiento en la evaluación por peso de puntos.
– Sáquele a su equipo de trabajo lo mejor en sus juntas de trabajo y haga que las decisiones sean las mejores para todos, su empresa, y el entorno.

Pruebe su capacidad administrativa al cristalizar sueños no alcanzados

JULIO CESAR IDROBO RENDÓN